AF405638

SEEKING THE LIGHT,

LESSONS LEARNED.

T.R. VILLARREAL

Dedication

To all who are on your own journey to seek
your light. Remember to do so with
passion, a kind heart, and with eyes
opened wide.

Table of Contents

Contents

Go Forth

Go forth my beautiful, lovely child.
Go and be brave and see the world.
It is the best teacher you will ever know.
Don't let your feet stay in one place too long.
Feet are meant to be moving.
So let yours move and jump and dance
to music only you can hear.

Learn to be bold and reckless
but not enough to hurt someone.
Regrets do not serve one well.
Seek answers to your questions
and always have questions to ask.
Listen more and speak less.
And when appropriate, always give your thanks.

Enjoy the minutes given you in this life
you will soon see how fleeting they can be.
Remember to give your love freely and often.
If true, there is no shame in loving someone.
Get your heart broken but never shattered.
Know that time heals everything, even hearts.
Although when it happens, it may not seem so.

Always be kind and thoughtful
even when kindness is not shown to you.
That is a fault of their own, not yours.
Keep hope in your heart always.
See the best in people if possible.
And if kindness is not extended to you,
go forth and move your feet to jump and dance
to a place in this world, where people will.

Why Suffer

What does it mean to suffer, to have pain in our heart?
What purpose does it serve one
to be visited by such cold cruelty?

Some would say it is God's punishment,
penance for a misdeed.
A pain inflicted as a lesson to be learned.

I prefer to think a God of love
can simply not be that unkind or cruel.
It may be more analogous to experiencing something beautiful.

Beauty is presented for one to appreciate and take in.
It is presented as a gift to the senses.
Meant to touch your mind and emotion.

So it is with suffering.
Know it is presented as a gift to you.
A necessary and unwelcome lesson to be learned,

about compassion and empathy and kindness
toward those who also suffer within their own existence.
For us to understand, no one should have to suffer alone.

And so it is, that unfortunately,
our own compassion, our empathy, comes at a cost,
meant to be understood on a very personal level.

For it is from our own suffering that springs
the understanding, the empathy, the compassion
toward the suffering of others.

My Woods

At this stage in my life,
I often slip back in time, at lease in my mind.
I am back in my woods behind the house
surrounded by climbing cliffs, trees and brush all around.

The birds sing and lizards scurry up the trees
as I walk the well trod paths. I know them all.
My slingshot in my back pocket
and my small knife with its wood like handle
made of plastic tucked into my well worn and turned up jeans.

I am in my safe place,
nothing or no one to bother me.
and still, not quite far enough away from my mother's voice
and when she calls me to come in to eat.

To me, it feels as if I am in a far away world.
I am alone, the only one for miles around.
In truth, my woods were all of a block in length
bounded by the tracks to one side
and the housing projects, where we lived on the other.

This the place where my imagination knew no bounds.
Where scenes from Treasure Island, Tom Sawyer,
Don Quixote and Great Expectations, spoke to me and came to life.
This was the place I ran to when I would say to my mother,
"horita vengo", and would not return home until the sun set.

I would come into the house, filthy and sweating
a necklace of dirt around my neck.
Joining the rest of the family to supper
to eat what was presented, except frijoles, to my father's consternation.

After, I would open the latest book assigned from school
which my kind hearted teacher would allow me
to bring it home.
To read what adventures awaited me
when next I would visit my woods.

Someone Who I Loved

My mind constantly goes to someone who I loved
and love still gone now many years
and yet I still vividly remember
how she walked and how she talked
how she simply made me smile.

and though I get along well now
many years after
she continues to fill my heart
not surprising after all

it was she who was my first friend
my first teacher, my mother
the one who most of all
provided protection even as I feigned protestation

The memory of her will never leave me
I don't want it to I welcome the thought of her knowing
it was she who provided and continues to do so
all I need to get along and be a part of this
sometimes cold and sometimes cruel and
yet kind and wonderful world.

Her Family and Her Garden

I could see her from the kitchen window
wearing that old weathered straw hat she always wore
bending down to her beloved garden

she would take each tiny lettuce seed
from her fragile trembling hand

and like a precious tiny jewel placing it in just the right spot
where the soil remained slightly moist
and the sun would warm it and keep it safe and happy

The strength and energy which she once possessed
had left her years ago

and so like her family she loved
could never even think of abandoning either

In her mind her family and her garden
required her love and tending and she was prepared
to give both as much as required to flourish

for to her, they were both much the same
each demanded and received her unconditional love

she knew that as her vegetables and her children grew
strong and straight in their own way
both would never fail to give the same to her.

Show Them

We are here but for a brief period in time.
The best we can do, in that time,
for those we love and treasure
is to show them how much
in both words and deeds.
They will certainly appreciate it
and just as important, so will you.

Persistence Has Its Place

It all comes back to you,
yes it always comes back to you.
I knew from the start
that you had the key to my heart.
It doesn't take an Einstein or Touring
to figure out how I felt about you.
No need to break a cipher
to know I was out to overpower your resistance
and hesitancy.

My mission in life was to win you over.
To make you mine.
To let you realize I am the one for you
and you are the one for me.
Your task is to simply see me and hear me
and let me love you
and let me convince you
to give up and let me have you.
Because in matters of the heart, and science,
even Einstein and Touring would agree,
persistence has its place.

Goodbye

When you love someone,
sometimes the hardest word
to hear is "Goodbye".
Every time it is said, it takes a bite.
And it's those small but punishing
bites that accumulate into major wounds.
Until a life is left drained and spent.
With no hope for tomorrow,
and no viable sense of what is to be.

This is what your goodbyes do to me
and so when you say it
know that even if you see no blood
the wound is still there festering
with despair and loss.
And every time you leave,
that nonbleeding wound
just grows deeper and more profound
even if you can't see it when you return.

Adiós

Cuando amas alguien,
a veces pienso que la palabra más difícil
de escuchar es "Adiós".
Cadavez que se dice, se da un mordisco.
Y son esos pequeños pero castigadores
mordiscos los que se acumulan en heridas importantes.
Hasta que una vida se agota y se gasta.
Sin esperanza para mañana
y sin un sentido viable de lo que será.

Esto es lo que me hacentus despedidas
y, por lo tanto, cuando lo digas, debes
saber que, incluso si no ves sangre,
la herida sigue allí enconada
de desesperación y pérdida.
Y cada vez que te vas,
esa herida que no sangra se ve
hace cada vez más profunda,
incluso si no puedes verla, cuando regresas.

The Loss Was Mine

I remember the exact time,
the exact place,
when I broke her heart.
It was raining outside
the rain running down the panes of glass
like the tears on her face.
I knew I was much too honest
when she asked if I cared for her?
Did I have feeling for her
as she did for me?
My response was less than callous
when I replied that I loved her
but I was simply not in love with her.
She knew exactly what I meant.
How I wish I had said it differently
not so cold or so cruel.
With tears flowing,
and her head in her hands,
she quietly whispered,
"is there anything I could do differently
or say something to make you change your mind"?
Looking into her tear filled eyes
and reaching for her hand
I simply said "No".
Reaching for the door
she walked out into the pouring rain
and from that day forward
we never spoke again.
The irony or karma as life tends to teach
from all that was said and done,
was the realization that the loss was purely and deservedly
mine.

Night Time

At night they come to haunt me.
Feeling I am falling into the abyss
deeper and deeper.
It seems as if I am lost forever in my own head.
And then I awake from this discomforting nightmare
to find you next to me in our bed.
Your arm across my chest
and your head resting on my shoulder.
The smell of your soft hair
perfuming the air I am breathing.
And I know all will be fine.
You continue sleeping.
Not knowing what you do for both my body and soul.
And so I reach for you to hold you closer
content in the comfort and joy you bring to my life.
Pulling me back from the abyss.
Knowing I am embraced in your love and being.

The Sun

Walking out to my garden
I see what is growing
and I raise my voice and sing to the sacred shining sun
to say thank you
for assisting and allowing
my crops and flowers to grow and flourish
there is no escaping the sacred connection
between what grows
and the light the sun shines upon.

It is a gift from the gods
to know it is the sun
that provides the light
and the warmth
that makes plants lush and green
so it is only fitting and appropriate
to say thank you for the miracle
that is the sun as it caresses the earth,
and wraps it in its warmth
and showers it with such abundant love and kindness.

Home

I am finally coming home.
Home is where all that I love is,
where life starts and begins and ends.
Where all memories lie,
where the last mystery is explained.

Surrounded by the tastes and sounds and sights of life
that have all the meanings that matter.
It is the music and muses and the wonderful movements.
It is all the best of what it is to live when there is no more breath.

Think of chocolate and champagne.
Think of Vivaldi and the sublime and glorious reach of his
Winter,
the Beatles and Dylan, Beethoven and the Talking Heads,
and the tender emotions wrought by Mariachi music.

It is dungeness crab dipped in butter, bought from Race Street
Fish.
It is the writings of Whitman, Dickens, Sandberg, and Steinbeck.
It is the works of Rivera and Frida, Picasso and Calder.

It is the sense and scent of making love.
Running fingers over velvety soft smooth skin.
It is lovely eyes looking back at you saying I love you.
It is the creation of a beautiful child.
It is the rapturous bliss of being.

It is a place without religion, without regulations, without dogma,
without deacons, or priests, monks, or imams.
It is a wonderful place
in endless time and space.
It is that place where all love's longings come to pass.

Gone Away

Another hard winter has come and gone away,
and now, Spring is on the way.
And maybe we can breathe again.
And maybe we can live again.
Without the constant worry,
without the worrisome pain.

A new season on the way
to move ahead without looking back
to what was or what might have been.
One thing we know for sure,
tomorrow will come.
Giving us a reason to breathe and live again.

Yes, some goals were set aside and some dreams deferred.
And of course, loved ones' lives cut short.
It is only proper and fitting to remember.
But let the sorrow and sadness be soothed
by living your life good and well.
And to remember, a new season is on the way.

After Death

Some would say, after death comes to claim me
I will no longer be of this world
or any world.

There will simply be no more me
no more you or
no more we.

Just as before birth,
there is no existence
so it is in death.

In knowing this,
I must admit,
there comes a certain kind of comfort.

However, in truth,
I must confess,
in my heart, I only wish it were not so.

Every Morning

Every morning she begins
stationed before her mirror.
Like an artist with palette and brushes
she begins to create her grand self illusion.
First, the foundation on which to work.
Next, the curve of the eyebrows, just so.
Then the cheeks, pronounced and high.
On to her lips, sensuous and red.
She stands slightly back to see herself.
She is pleased in her look, not realizing
all she needs is the radiance of her smile
and her confidence within,
to project her true and lasting beauty.

Happiness

Happiness can come upon one even when alone
and it can be glorious and gracious in its gift
but you will learn that some moments of happiness
can be much more glorious and gracious
when shared with someone you love.

Those times become moments of remembrance
mutual memories of sharing and caring
and seeing things through other's eyes
becoming moments of happiness compounded
and at their best, much more glorious when shared.

First A Glance

It was a short period of time.
In between one and onto another,
when she appeared.
First a glance, then a hello.
Later we talked just nonsense
over Sake in a local Japanese place with a bar.

We didn't know it was so late
until they wanted to close.
But I didn't want it to end.
That's when I knew,
that what I sought was right here
in front of me, saying goodbye.

Reluctantly, I said goodbye
and she walked to her car.
I did glance her way,
Not wanting to be obvious in my gaze.
but the way she confidently walked away became seared in my
memory leaving me breathless, with anticipation
and wanting to know her more.

Dance With Me

Come dance with me one last time
before you leave, before you say goodbye.
Let me hold you close in my arms.
Let me see into your dark brooding eyes.

As I come to understand what I will miss
for the rest of my waking days.
Wishing I could tell you " I love you"
one last time.

We do not need to talk
if you wish not to.
Just let us move with the music
with you in my arms, like many times before.

Allow me to smell that perfume that is you
and the warm softness of your hand in mine
and think about our time spent together
chasing our dreams and chasing each other.

When tomorrow comes and I awake
knowing you are gone
and my bed is empty
please know, I hope you continue chasing your dreams.

I will do the same, perhaps with a little more hesitation
somewhat changed, I am sure.
Taking meager solace in knowing that I loved you once,
and you loved me.

Knowing that even as change comes,
in my life, the love you gave
made all the difference.

I Wish For You

All I wish for you is a million dreams.
Dreams of beauty and bliss and wonder.
Dreams to help you in your sleep
and soothe your thoughts and keep you safe.

And as you sleep remember
I will never be far
to make sure you are safe and sound
I will always be around.

Close your eyes and let me
join you in your dreams
and we can walk and talk
and be together once again.

And as you wake
know that I was with you
to watch you in your sleep
to keep you safe and sound.

Abide By Me

Abide by me, for a little longer
abide by me and hear my plea
Listen close and let me pause
to choose my words wisely.

And when I finish you can decide
if you will stay.
Know this,

since we have shared the same space
every day I awoke to your gorgeous face
and see you move from our bed to the bath
watching your every lovely sensuous step

minutes later, coming out
your long flowing hair pinned back
face scrubbed and makeup free
no one could look more beautiful

moving to the kitchen
to fix your Earl Grey and two slices of toast
balancing each as you decide
what to wear for the day

asking me which I like or no
and of course, saying yes to everything
because I knew that everything you wore
was simply wonderful on you.

and you would smile
a smile of confidence and assurance
because secretly you knew I was right
but much too modest to say in words

seeing you dressed
saying goodbye with a sweet and gentle kiss
and out the door
to meet the new day

leaving me longing for you
and the wonderful warmth of you in my bed once again and
wishing it will always be that way.

Without A Heart

Maybe on another day,
maybe another place,
I would be there for you.

Not this day though,
nor this place
it's way too late for you

to even ask
or me to even think
of doing so.

The thing is
you left long ago
and took my heart when you did.

Since your leaving
I have turned cold and cruel
and uncaring.

So of course, my answer must be no.
It is the inevitable consequence and the penance to be paid
for leaving me without a heart.

Eres

Qué más puedo decirte
eres mi corazón
la alma de mi vida
no me hagas sufrir mas.

Necesito tu pasión y tu calor
como alguien necesita aire para vivir.
No soy nada sin tu cuerpo a mi lado.
No soy nada sin tus besos dulce.

Tu eres la Trinidad en mi vida
mi propósito, mi vida y mi amor.
Soy menos que nada sin ti.
Simplemente polvo soplando en el viento.

You Are

What more can I tell you?
You are my heart,
the soul in my life,
do not make me suffer more.

I need your passion and your warmth
as someone needs air to live.
I am nothing without your body by my side.
I am nothing without your sweet kisses.

You are the trinity in my life
my purpose, my life, and my love.
I am less than nothing without you.
Merely dust blowing in the wind.

Bliss

Bliss, for me, is those times
when I hold you in my arms
tight against my body, in a warm embrace.
And I can feel you breathe
and hear your soft sighs.

No need for words.
No need to say a thing.
Nothing but sweet heartfelt, I love you's
whispered in your ear,
that only you and I can hear.

Felicidad

La felicidad, para mí, son esos momentos
en los que te sostengo en mis brazos
contra mi cuerpo en un cálido abrazo.
Y puedo sentirte respirar
y escuchar tus suaves suspiros.

No necesito palabras.
No hace falta decir nada.
Nada más que dulce corazón, te amo,
susurró en tu oído,
que solo tú y yo podemos escuchar.

Blue

When I am feeling blue
and I don't have you for comfort
I have a beer and shed a tear
and curse the fate
that brought me here, without you.

And if you don't return
I promise I will burn
all the pages and pages of poetry
I wrote for you. And no one but me will ever know
how you were loved, and what we both went through.

And as each page of my book for you is turned
and I watch it slowly burn.
I will quickly learn.
That life is not always fair
and you don't always need a flame to get burned.

Mortality

It is our mortality
that should serve as incentive
to live.

For in knowing
we are all destined to die
should cause us to live
and to love,
as if life will never end.

Like Seeds

Like seeds, we rise from the soil
up into the sun.
We are sons and daughters of the earth.
Well before there was an America
we were here ruling men
and the creatures of the jungle.
Building structures and creating art
no one could dream of.
Our Gods were the Sun and the Moon
and the Stars.

And then they came who said they were Shepherds
for God. We knew that was not so.
For they did not smell of sheep.
They smelled of gluttony and disease
and of the horses, they rode.
They did not carry staffs, but swords.

And they came, who said they
worshiped only one God
but that God was gold and riches.
We learned too late it seems
that their belief in a single deity
was simply a pretense
to plunder and destroy and steal
what took eons to build.

But like seeds, we knew how to survive
and we rose then and rise still
to be nourished and warmed by the Sun.
For we are the true sons and daughters of Aztlan.

Atonement

He was asked did he have any regrets
is there something that must be atoned?
A question he had never been asked.
And so he thought and thought
believing after a life well lived and well experienced
there must be something.

Something that requires and needs confession and penance?
His Catholic upbringing and beliefs
long since abandoned, of course, came again to haunt him.
Guilt is such a strong and profound emotion
it can gnaw one to the bone.
Like a punch to the gut, guilt can simply bring you to your
knees.

In that split second, a seared and long-forgotten memory
stabbed at his heart.
His mother, long since gone, crying at the window.
He could see her clearly like it was yesterday.
Crying, with her hands to her face, sighing deeply.
All he knew, all he could remember, of those
gut-wrenching tears were because of something he had done.

Had he come to her to beg forgiveness, to say, I am sorry?
Suddenly, that recollection brought tears to his own eyes
and he had to look away.
He heard the question repeated, did he have any regrets?
"Yes", he answered in a soft voice, "I made my mother cry,
and for that, there can never be forgiveness nor atonement".

To Save A Soul

Come in through the double doors,
into the quiet and the dark.
Let the smoke and smell of the incense encircle you
in its wonderful embrace.
Deposit your coins, light a candle.
And say your prayer for the dead.

Sometimes, it is all
that can be or need be done
to save a soul.

In ancient times,
when other superstitions ruled,
the Ferryman was paid
two coins for passage
across the river Styx, into the underworld.

Either way, just in case,
keep some coins at the ready
in your pocket or your purse.
And don't forget some
smooth round stones.

For while flowers at a grave have their place.
They like a life, fade and then die.
But a stone for remembrance, placed at the grave
has a permanence like a lasting memory.
And a soul, if it is to be saved,
needs to be remembered.
And made a lovely lasting memory.

To Her, I Turn

I loved her from afar
circumstances dictated that it be so
estranged from the land where I was born
I left to seek my dreams in a place more accommodating
more accepting of what I sought
she remained there for the rest of her life
and so it was only if she visited
or I visited her that we could be together
and when that happened it was as if
we were never apart
conversations flowed with no pregnant pauses
we were easy and relaxed with each other
she was my touchstone she kept me grounded
she knew me better than I knew myself
whatever I achieved I achieved with her
always on my mind always on my mind
never wanting to be a burden
I strove and stretched wanting only to make her smile
and when sometimes life held me down
it was to her I turned to cry
and she would listen and understand
and always say exactly what I needed to hear
never once did she abandon me
for it was not in her nature to do so
even when I gave her cause

later our visits became more infrequent
for it seemed we met only at
births, baptisms or funerals
It is the inevitability of later years
that this becomes so
it was in the last funeral that we parted
for it was hers
and in the sorrow and the sadness
of her leaving
I came to understand I would never
ever be alone
for even in her parting
I knew her love for me would always go on
and so it is to her
I still turn.

Grace For The Good

There once was a time when
everyone looked to the West
for guidance and grace for the good.
It was the natural and common sense
thing to do.

Compassion, character, and intelligence from our leaders
were values to be admired.
Doing the best for the common good
was a worthy pursuit.
Leaving no one behind was the lodestar.

Within the blink of an eye,
and asleep at the wheel,
we are faced with children in cages,
and America too full for the immigrant
seeking her dream. Lying is no longer a liability.

We see American cities crumbling in decay.
Americans suffering for lack of medical care,
children worried over climate change
and wondering if their schools are safe.
We value guns over feeding the poor and hungry.

Is this what is meant by "Make America Great Again"?
America has always had the capacity for greatness.
For we have the greatest and most potent weapon
to facilitate meaningful change:
Democracy and the value of an individual's right to choose!

Exercise your own choice with caution and care.
Exercise it with thought and diligence.
And with the knowledge that in the blink of an eye,
we can make America the hope and dream of the world
once again.

A Wish For Us

We are all men and women mortal, are we not?
We all breathe and all in our own time, die.
Then why do most of us live as if life is forever?
Can we not extend to each a knowing hand of understanding?

All of us who live through this world
acquire our own faults and frailties along the way.
And yes, along the way if so blessed,
acquire the values and virtues we cherish in others.

Among our friends and brethren, we wish only the best.
Among our children and loved ones, we wish love and
happiness.
To our fellow men and women who live on this good green
earth,
we should wish only as much as we wish for ourselves.

It is only fitting that we do.
For to do otherwise would secure our own demise.
We the human race are capable of so much,
capable of achieving amazing, spectacular, and wondrous
things.
Let us all, each in our own way, work to do so, before we take
our last breath.

It Is

I am a better man
because of you and what you taught me
about love and life and acceptance.
It is you who provides
my energy, my motivation, my compassion.

When you slide your hand in mine
I know you are mine and I am yours.
When you smile and I see your gorgeous eyes
invariably you melt my less than tender heart.

You are the reason that life
has a purpose and a meaning.
You are the music and melody
only I can hear.

It is your beautiful mind and your beautiful face
and the rapturous way about you
that provides all I ever need,
all I would ever want, to make my life worth living.

There is really no other reason.
And so when I say, "I love you",
you and I know exactly what
that truly means.

Never, Ever Just One Thing

To be honest, in retrospect, he couldn't tell you he knew
her.
He thought they were friends and sometimes lovers.
But to her, it seems it simply stopped at friends, if that.
It stayed that way until it didn't.

And of course, things never stay the same.
Change happens, sometimes for the good, sometimes not.
In this case for the not. He wanted her more and more,
and she was of a different mind.

What he forgot is that for one to be friends or more
that decision is for two to make.
He just thought it would be the next progression
thinking they were on the same page, she was on to the
next chapter.

And so, as they sometimes say, drift happens
and separation follows.
He stayed onshore grounded.
And she sailed away with full sails billowing in the wind.

Never looking back, like a ghost she disappeared past the
fog.
His fog never quite lifted. Wallowing in self-doubt and self-
pity.
Recovery was in slow motion but time passing allowed the
return to some semblance of normalcy.

And normalcy is to understand no person is never, ever,
just one thing.
To think otherwise, is to live at your own peril.

Love Does Not Follow Labels

Why is it so hard to accept the inescapable?
Love does not follow labels.
It does not adhere to any rigid definition or dogma.

How can love be condemned
simply because it follows
no acceptable script?

It is for the lovers and the loved
to be who they are
and simply follow their heart.

How can it be a sin
to merely love and be loved?
Such would be a cruel and cold world.

No need to weaponize labels or definitions
It serves merely to separate and ostracize
and to cause such callous damage and anguish.

The God I have come to know,
that is part of my heart,
has no such intentions.

Love is a precious gift given,
meant to be welcomed and received with grace. If one is so
inclined.
There is simply no choice in the matter.

Everything Will Be Fine

I can still hear her now
everything will be fine.
everything will work out, you will see.
just tend to your garden and plant your seeds
and stand back and be prepared to see a miracle.

It is the miracle of life
prepare the soil, give it water
give it your love your time and attention
and let nature take its course
nature understands what it takes
for life to begin and flourish and to end.

It is much the same with children
give them your love your time and attention
prepare their way and teach them well
stand back and be prepared to see a miracle

the miracle of a life
just let nature take its course
nature knows what it takes
for life to begin, to flourish, and to end.

Knowing you did so
will provide a semblance of sanity and solace
understanding you did your best
in assisting nature in its miracle making.

And everything will be fine.

After You Got To Know Him

After you got to know him
one could detect a certain melancholy.
It was apparent in the way he walked
and certainly in the way he talked and spoke to others.

It was not off-putting
for there was a gentle way about him.
Of someone who had seen much of the world
and experienced what it is to live and love.

You could imagine his choice or choices
in love had not gone his way
and it showed in his manner
and demeanor in how he spoke of life.

The grey on his temples
and the small but deep lines along his eyes
and the tiny tremors of his fingers
showed a life of unresolved worries.

His smoking and how he held his scotch
one in each hand showed
a man of lingering and unquenched habits.
Perhaps an indication of small or large battles carried over.

Still, there was no doubt
that one could learn much
by simply being in his presence
and simply listening as he talked.

He was a man of many stories
and one could see a hard history written on his face.
If one wondered as to his musical likes
you would not be far off if you guessed jazz and Chet Baker.

Listen carefully and you would hear
stories of love and loss
of monies made and squandered
of being lost and found.

He would speak of two kinds of knowledge.
The kind you learn in living life yourself.
And the kind you learn from others' mistakes.
Both of which offered much of value.

He would say never be afraid to make love
and make it often.
There can never be regret in making too much love.
Allow tender memories to be made and tender mercies given.

Seek the truth in yourself and others
and if it does not come
maybe it is time to move on
and seek it in others and certainly in yourself.

Life is much too short
and much too valuable to waste.
Life is for the living to experience.
For whenever it comes, you will know that death is but a short
span away.
And as it must, it inevitably and eventually came to stop for him.
So when I listen to Chet Baker now
I can see that old man still
Sitting, a cigarette in one hand and a scotch in the other,
listening to Chet and smiling.

A Beautiful Way About Her

She would come but never overstay.
She would always say, I want people to miss me when I leave
and of course, we always did.
She was like a bright light, banishing the darkness
and leave us smiling with her stories and her mere presence.

She had a beautiful way about her
and the way she moved around a room was simply dazzling.
It was not an exaggeration to say it was impossible not to notice her.
In a room full of people, she was the one your eyes followed.
And as she glided about the room she would leave the lovely scent of
her perfume.

I never knew if she actually realized how beautiful she was
but those of us her friends and lovers certainly did.
There was a beguiling strength about her that served her well
in those times when either men or women would conspire
or attempt to get closer than she would allow.

There are those among us and we know who we are,
who believe that if one is beautiful and dazzling and friendly
it is simply an invitation for other things.
While she was all these things, she would quickly
dissuade you of any such thoughts unless she was of the same mind.
for while she was no prude, natural boundaries were still observed.

And common courtesies and appropriate manners were to be expected.
Being a woman of the world did not mean one would accept all
invitations.
That was the environment she lived in and it had served her very well.
And she would simply not accept anything less.

To outside observers, yes, she was beautiful and a wonderful
conversationalist.
To those of us fortunate to be her friend she was all that and more.
Smart and kind and thoughtful and compassionate to a fault.

And when you became her friend, even after being her lover,
you knew she would stand with you. But it was her kind and tender
heart
that made all the difference and separated her from all the rest.

To Not Ask

I spent much of my life in absolute confusion.
What does it mean to live?
Why does the songbird sing and the human dance?
Does life have a purpose and who or what provides it?

Now, after all these years of living,
the questions still persist, so, so many.
And some will never be answered
but that is no reason not to ask.

Curiosity is the catalyst,
the crucible on which answers are provided and proved.
To not ask is not to care.
And not caring is no life at all.

For as long as men and women live,
men and women will ask.
And learning becomes the result
and it is learning that can lead to a life well-lived.

Eternal Song

This is the eternal song I sing.
When it seems all hope is gone.
When life appears to hold one down
in a dark and dreary place.

Stand up and hold your head up
and let all know, and proclaim that you are here.
For nothing and no one can keep you down,
hope springs from within your own heart.

It springs from the knowledge of your own worth.
For the God or Gods who made you
would not have done so
knowing you were incapable of contributing to this world.

So sing your own eternal song of self-worth.
Sing it loud and proud for all to hear.
We are all children of the same God
imbued from inception, with the same budding talents.

We merely wait for you
in your own way, in your own time, to set them free
and blossom in service to the world,
and in service to us all.

Never Quite the Same

The time she said it, it was almost midnight
we were walking through the Plaza de Cesar Chavez.
Turning to me with my hand in hers
she whispered I think I love you.

At first, I said nothing.
First mistake.
Seconds later, I replied
you don't love me, you don't even know me.

And suddenly, second mistake.
I could see her lovely smile leave her
and she looked at the ground
and released her hand from mine.

In that instant, I had doubted her.
Imagine the strength it took
for her to say those words.
How ungracious and cavalier I was in response.

From that time to now
things between us
have never been quite the same.
And of course, I know why.

It was my own fear and apprehension
at hearing those frightening words
"I think I love you", and what that meant
would not allow me to accept her heartfelt words.

And in my less than noble retreat
I lost her trust and confidence. I lost that look of love in her eyes.
I knew it was the beginning of the end
and I realized I would never hear those words from her again.

Open and Inviting

Waking up
and walking into the kitchen
I see the package of dark chocolate Oreos
open and inviting

I take one
and eat it
delicious as it melted
in my warm mouth

it was all I could do
to leave you some
but I did
and I know you know why.

Choices and Change

Sitting in the dark
nursing my scotch
listening to Marvin's lament
I can hear it and feel it
and live it.

"I want you, but I want you to want me too".
Tell it, brother.
Let it flow.
Pour it into me. Finally, I understand.
Only Marvin can save me now.

Life can be so cruel, after being so good
for so long.
Someone once said: "Life offers
only two things, choices and change".
I have found, unfortunately, both can be sometimes, bitter sweet

It Was Meant To Be

From the very beginning, she was easy to know
and easier to look at
her golden eyes seemed to see right through you
seemingly knowing exactly what you felt.

And so it was natural to go under her spell.
Not by accident or coincidence
no, it was meant to be.
Fate played its mystery and I was lost.

And so began a self-imposed adventure
a lovely journey, a trip I could not foresee.
Like all journeys, it had its breaks, detours,
and sometimes drama.

Yet, we got past all that and survived
to know one another even better. To be equals in love and life.
To know that if one is to love
one must learn to accept and forgive.

She made it easy, me not so much.
But she stayed and for that, I was always grateful.
Truth is I could not imagine my life without her,
without her golden eyes, her smile, her mere presence.

My heart was hers and I readily acknowledged it,
to her, and the Gods that made her.
She was my gift.
I was more than pleased for the gift that was her.

Each night before we slept
she was always and remains so, in my prayer of thanks.
And upon her insistence, with no argument from me,
two kisses, one for her and one for me.

It Is Enough To Know

Have you ever wondered
does fate make your life
or does life choose your fate?
Who is to know?

It is enough to know
that life is to be lived, not abandoned.
Give it your heart and live it well and true
and it will surely be true to you.

Have no illusions, life can sometimes be hard
and challenging and often cruel.
Take solace in the knowledge it is sometimes so
to make one think.

To learn and embrace those times when it is not. When it
presents love and joy and revelry and sheer beauty.
For surely in every life that is so. Even in times of doubt and
dismay, there is much to commend it.

A life is to be celebrated.
Appreciate whatever comes.
It is yours and yours alone
and surely worth the living.

When Spring Came

When Spring came. you would see her
with flowers in her long brown hair
and gold bangles on her wrists
and little stars dangling from her ears.

She never came to understand
how truly beautiful she was
just by walking along the sand.
Her tan legs glowing
and her smile showing
like a lovely dream.

Every day I would run to the beach
hoping to see her.
Some days brought only disappointment
On others, pure exaltation at seeing her.

I was never bold enough to approach
or even say hello.
She was older and simply unattainable.
Was she real, or a figment of my imagination?
I was merely pleased to see her from afar
in her little white spring dress, hugging every curve.

Three Springs came and went,
and I always pleased and content
to see her with those flowers in her hair
and her long brown hair flowing.
Her tan legs showing, walking along the sand.

Years later, I came to know
what a lovely memory she made.
Of her, it could truly be said
she was the stuff of which
poems are written and winsome memories made.

I Wish For You

All I wish for you is a million dreams.
Dreams of beauty and bliss and wonder.
Dreams to help you in your sleep
and soothe your thoughts and keep you safe.

And as you sleep remember
I will never be far
to make sure you are safe and sound
I will always be around.

Close your eyes and let me
join you in your dreams
and we can walk and talk
and be together once again.

And as you wake
know that I was with you
to watch you in your sleep
to keep you safe and sound.

For if you remember when last we spoke
I made this promise.
You would see me in your dreams
to keep you always, always safe and sound.

Her Kiss

Hers were the kisses I remember.
They were like no others,
gentle and soft and passionately pure.
Kissing her was like getting lost
in the most encompassing and compassionate drug.
Where nothing or no one except she
was present.
Not a thing existed save her mouth on mine.

Even now, just the thought of her
stirs me beyond comprehension
beyond nothing else but her.
Seems strange, or not so much
when I remember the effect she had on me.
How the touch of her lips on mine
was capable of making me lost in the magic
of her lips, mouth, and tongue.

It was only when the kisses stopped
and my drug of choice was gone
that I realized it would never be the same.
Gone was the magic only she
was capable of making.
And as the pain of withdrawals and the shakes set in
there was no one but me to blame.

Sometimes, just sometimes, she would let you
get close enough to allow you
to get lost in her eyes.
That's all it would take.
Even before a soft touch
or tender kiss.

Without a word from you,
she would know she possessed you totally.
Suddenly, you would want what
you never knew you needed
and you would need
what you never wanted.

On your part, you never felt lost.
How could you?
You were under the special magic spell
that was her eyes, her smile
and the gorgeous way about her.

Being lost in her was the least
of your worries.
It was the separation anxiety you felt
at not being with her.
In not holding her
or kissing her.
In not hearing her laugh.

In time, you came to understand
that anxiety would never leave you.
And as long as that feeling was there
you knew she would be too.
It was the price one had to pay
for the pleasure of being lost in her eyes,
in her smile,
and the gorgeous way about her.

Do I Still Touch Your Heart

Tell me please, do I still touch your heart?
Or has too much time passed between us?
Are the words, I love you, insufficient
to make a difference?

I recall a time, when a tender touch would suffice
to bring you near and let my arms bring you even closer.
It was a time when the passion and the pursuit
was enough to stir the heart.

Now, we are both left with the remnants
of recollections and memories.
Of what was and what was not to be.
It is the sorrow and sadness of time passing.

The Gods can give and take away
with no regards to the consequences of either.
Life is sometimes made of pleasures and pains
and in this instance, life gave us an abundance of both.

One takes and one gives
not necessarily in that order.
But how much one gives or takes
can make all the difference.

For us, it is enough to know we knew love.
To know we knew each other.
And that the remnants of recollections of each other
can still bring us smiles.

See Heaven

To those who wish to see a small piece of heaven
we need only look into the eyes of those we love
there you will see it in its purest form
reflected back at you
all those lovely feelings
of being protected and cared
of being enveloped in a nurturing embrace
of knowing you are loved
by one who wants only what you want and need
even when you don't even see it in yourself.

Simple Things and Simple Gifts

Sitting next to an open window
the breeze coming in to say hello
bringing its night perfume,
orange blossoms and new-mown grass.

In the house, Copeland's Appalachian Spring is playing
painting a picture of America.
I pause and stop to listen
as it stirs the heart of even the heartless.

It is the story in music, we all long for.
Where men and women are moved
to achieve great and wonderful things.
It is the hope and optimism of an American people.

Given so much that we sometimes forget
to look out the window
and see the majesty and magic of the night
and take in the fragrance of its lovely perfume.

Sometimes, it is the simple things and simple gifts
of this earth and this existence
that is enough to move the heart, stir the soul
and lead us to understand, the best is yet to be.

When we simply stop to pause and to listen and to see.

Borne High

It is only proper and right this man should be borne high above
on strong shoulders, loyal and true.
It should be so and well deserved
for the years of devoted self-sacrifice and service he rendered
to family, friends, and all he encountered.

Let us never forget that this man, in spite of all he endured,
rose well above many in his accomplishments and
achievements
even in the face of so many obstacles meant to hold one down.
He persevered and made a difference in the lives he touched.
And so as we weep, let us also rejoice in knowing him.

In this, his final goodbye, let it be known
that for a person of honor, integrity, kindness, and compassion
it is only fitting that such a person as he should be lifted high.
So that all who knew him shall see his spirit and sanctified soul
and recognize him and weep at the loss of his leaving.

Carry My Bones

When my time comes
and there is no longer anything left to win
and nothing more to prove and I am dead and done
carry my bones to the pyre

and light the fire and make it bright
and let the smoke fly up high
taking my spirit and soul straight up in the sky
where only the stars shine and the eagles soar

so that my people may know there is nothing more
to say about me than the flaming fire
and towering swirling smoke has to say.

I Am Who I Am

I was cleansed in the river Jordan
to no avail.
Baptized by the Franciscans and Jesuits.
And yet, I remain like a child confused, seeking answers.

I am who I am, suffering from a crisis of the heart.
A creature, same as you, of the same God.
Trying only to do good
and follow my moral compass.

If anyone is to blame for my flaws and failings,
blame God for he is my maker
and my example.
The path I follow had long ago been fated.

The life I live,
I lived following that path.
Of course, if sometimes I strayed,
it was simply because the light in me grew dim.

As I grew older and my eyesight declined
I noticed the path charted for me grew brighter
and so I hewed to the path set before me
with more passion, courage, and determination.

One could say that with my years
in decline and slipping away
one's focus on what lies ahead
simply became more pronounced and intense.

Or could it be simply a message
from the God who made us all?
Do not waste the years remaining you,
straying from your well-laid, well-lit path.
You need only look to the light.

A Longing Not Yet Achieved

After the life, he lived, well and good,
he could never understand
why on occasion, he was overwhelmed
by sadness and deep despair.

He knew he was loved
and he had loved.
From his many travels and his many experiences,
he had seen the beauty of this world.

And yet, he was puzzled
by this unexplained sense of incompleteness.
The sense of something missing.
It gnawed at his heart and soul.

Of course, after reflection and some searching
he came to understand.
This world of human beings
was one of haves and have nots.

The dream of equality and justice for all
was still that, merely a dream.
Something he worked for all his life
and longed for all
had yet to be achieved for so many of this world.

It is this longing of men and women
for justice and equality not yet achieved
that cleaved at his heart.
For without those attributes applied to all,
there can be no rest or solace for those who know what it is
to have them and to live, while so so many, live without,